The Lord's Prayer

An Interpretation by
RALPH W. SOCKMAN

Design and illustrations by Jean Penland

ABINGDON PRESS

NEW YORK   NASHVILLE

THE LORD'S PRAYER

Library of Congress Catalog Card Number: 62-14669

PRINTED AND BOUND BY THE PAR-
THENON PRESS, AT NASHVILLE, TEN-
NESSEE, UNITED STATES OF AMERICA

Our Father, who art in heaven, hallowed be
thy Name. Thy kingdom come. Thy will be done,
on earth as it is in heaven. Give us this day
our daily bread. And forgive us our trespasses, as
we forgive those who trespass against us. And
lead us not into temptation, but deliver us from evil.
For thine is the kingdom, and the power, and the
glory, for ever and ever. AMEN.

THE LORD'S PRAYER

THE LORD'S PRAYER IS THE MOST
important of all Christian documents. Almost
every Christian child commits it to memory.
Almost every service of Christian worship
includes it. Yet it comes trippingly on the
tongue and its clauses fall from our lips
without catching hold of our hearts. Its very
familiarity has dulled our spirits to the
fulness of its meaning.

Pause, therefore, and in your time of
reading examine the prayer anew. Follow the
movements of its thought and catch the
varied shades of its meaning. Through its
petitions one enters into communion with our
heavenly Father.

...the beauties of nature...
the love and laughter
of little children...

"And it came to pass, that, as he was praying
in a certain place,...one of his disciples
said unto him, Lord, teach us to pray, as John
also taught his disciples. And he said unto
them, When ye pray, say, Our Father."

We make bold to address thee, O God, as thy son Jesus hath taught us. In our homes we have learned to know our fathers and to count on their compassion. We have seen how they love and serve, how they work and suffer to give good things to their children. And we look to thee as the One who gave us our fathers and from whom they learned fatherhood. When we think of the blessings which thou hast bestowed upon us – the bounties of the good earth, the marvels of mind and body, the beauties of nature beyond the bare necessities, the fidelity of friends, the love and laughter of little children – when memory adds the treasures of the past to thy gifts of the present, we are led to call thee our Father. It is the highest and dearest name we know, embracing both father and mother and embodying both justice and mercy.

While we have not looked upon thy face
with our eyes, we have known One so holy and
altogether lovely that we believe him when
he said, "He that hath seen me hath seen the
Father." Ever since that One walked the
earth, worked here with his hands, lived among
the lowly, and laid down his life on a cross,
we feel that we know what thou, O God, art

like. Like his followers of the first century, we behold thy glory and goodness in the face of Jesus Christ. And so we draw near to thee with faith and without fear as children come home to a father. Having been taught that thou dost count the falling sparrows and look after the lost lambs, we somehow feel that no one of our lives is too little for thy concern, but that each of us is precious in thy sight, even as every child is dear to a parent. In love and trust we lay our petitions before thee, saying, "Our Father."

But Jesus thy son taught us to say, "Our Father, who art in heaven." We look up and

The earth is thine and the fulness thereof and all
that dwell therein.

remember that thou hast a whole universe
on thy hands. The earth is thine and the
fulness thereof and all that dwell therein.
The heavens declare thy glory and the

firmament showeth thy handiwork. When we consider the moon and the stars which thou hast ordained, who are we that thou shouldst be mindful of us? Where were we when thou didst lay the foundations of the earth? And why should we presume to ask for thy personal care when thou art the keeper of the seas and the sky? How canst thou control the stars and also keep thine eye on our little bodies? The question is too great for us.

Yet when we remember that thou hast made every star to differ from every other star and every leaf to be distinct from every other leaf and every man's fingertips to be so much his own that he can be found wherever he is hidden, it is not so hard to believe that each of us is known and watched by thee. Thy son was called the Good Shepherd who

knew his sheep by name, and when we think of
him we feel confident of thy never-ceasing
care. Thou dost seem so intimate in thy
nearness and yet so infinite in thy greatness.

When we look up to thee as "Our Father,
who art in heaven," the mystery of thy
love and the majesty of thy power impel us to

add, "Hallowed be thy Name." Like the
devout Hebrew children of old, we almost feel
that thy name is too sacred to be spoken
with our lips. We would be still and know
that thou art God. Our souls are hurt when
we hear thy name profaned by being taken
lightly and in vain as some do in cheap
and vulgar language. But we do long to talk
with thee in our lonely hours, and thy
name does sound lovely on the lips of little
children. We would be reverent toward
thee and yet not removed from thee.

   We bow in awe before thy mighty arm
which sendeth forth the lightnings and scattereth
the islands in the sea. Thy ways are higher

...and every leaf to be distinct from every other leaf and every man's fingertips to be so much his own...

than our ways as the heavens are high
above the earth. So we laud and magnify thy
glorious name, ever more praising thee
and saying, "Holy, holy, holy is the Lord of
hosts: the whole earth is full of his glory."

Yet through thy greatness so far above
us shines thy fatherly goodness so near unto
us that our awe is melted into reverence
and we pray, "Hallowed be thy Name."

When we turn from the stars which swing
so perfectly in the heavens and consider
the chaos in the movements of men, we are
aware that thou hast given man to have
dominion over a world which he cannot master
in his own strength. We know that thou
desirest also to sway the hearts of men because
thy son Jesus bade us to pray, "Thy kingdom
come. Thy will be done, on earth as it is
in heaven."

We have been erring children and have
run our courses in wayward paths. Thou hast
given us a bounteous earth, and we have

wasted its substance in riotous wars. Thou
hast made thy human creatures of one
blood to dwell as one family on all the face of
the earth, and we have set ourselves to
killing our brothers. Thou hast made our bodies
to be the temples of thy Holy Spirit, and
we have marred them with low temptations
and dark deeds. Our stubborn wills have
been unwilling to receive thy kingdom, yet our

hope of its coming does not die though the
earth has been drenched in blood and rumors of
wars are still heard in the land; for through
the torn and tangled threads of our troubled
lives we have glimpsed the pattern of thy
kingdom. We have caught intimations of what
the good life can be if we would live as
Jesus lived.

Thy son taught us that the kingdom of
heaven can be within us, and we have had days
when we felt it so. We have had times when
the peace which passeth all understanding stole
into our lives to calm our doubts and fears,
times when our noisy selfish strivings were

Thy ways are higher than our ways as the heavens are high above the earth.

silenced in the joy of serving thee, times when our stubborn wills yielded to the sway of thy sovereign love and our little rebellious souls found harmony and happiness in loyalty to thy spirit. Oh, yes, our

Father, bad as the world may seem to be,
we have had our good moments; and in our
highest hours we have found sufficient
evidence of thy kingdom within us to sustain
our faith in thy son's promise of its coming
around us.

Like the Christians of the first century, we
see not yet all things put under the feet
of Christ as King, but we see Jesus crowned
with glory and honor, for out of every
crisis and after every war his figure rises more
revered and adored. Men call him a dreamer
and turn from his precepts as impractical, but
out of the wreckage of their man-made
plans they rise to see that in Christ is the way,
the truth, and the life. Brute strength scorns
the cross of Jesus as a weapon of weakness, but
when wars have wrought their worst, we

wake up to realize that thy redeeming love is
the one power that never faileth. Because
all other roads lead to ruin, we have faith to
pray, "Thy kingdom come," believing that
in their lostness men will at last look toward
the light.

We human beings seem so perverse that
we persist in learning the hard way; but
through tribulation, peril, famine, and sword

we are learning that nothing can separate
us from thy love as revealed in Christ Jesus
our Lord. Slowly and never perfectly, but
yet surely and steadily, even governments are
beginning to see that peace on earth can
come only to men of good will and that the
kingdoms of this world can endure only as
their rule is fashioned after thy righteousness.

And, our Father, as we pray for thy
kingdom to come, grant us the grace to surrender
our wills to thy will. Make our vision clear
to see what thy wish is and our conscience clean
to do it. May we never from love of ease
decline the call of duty, nor for fear of shame
follow the crowd. We claim to be comrades

...but we see Jesus
crowned with glory
and honor...

of the Christ who in his Gethsemane prayed,
"Not my will but thine be done." Search
our hearts and strengthen our courage that we
may be able to say the same when our
choices are hard and the shadows are deep.

We know that we cannot ask for thy will to be done in the hours of crisis and in the wide affairs of earth unless we allow its work to begin in the smallest circles of our daily living. Keep us so constantly in thy company that we shall think thy thoughts after thee and learn to like the things which thou dost like. We would be faithful in our good intentions until they become fashioned into good habits and duty is lifted into desire. Not as idle watchers but as willing workers together with thee do we pray, "Thy kingdom come. Thy will be done, on earth as it is in heaven."

And now if we are to serve thee, our Father, as fellow workers in bringing thy kingdom to earth, we must have strength; and for this we ask, "Give us this day our daily bread."

We believe that all our needs are of concern to thee, for thou hast made us with these hungers and thirsts. Thy son came that we might have life and have it abundantly; and as the Great Physician he ministered both to the bodies and minds of men. He reminded us how thou dost feed the fowls of the air and clothe the grass of the fields; and he said that if we would seek first thy kingdom, our bodies would find enough for their needs through thy bounteous goodness. Help us so to set our hearts on thy goods that our hands may be guided toward the true goods of life and material possessions may cease to be the chief cause of our worry and strife.

When we pray, "Give us this day our daily bread," we do not expect thee to supply all our desires, for in our selfishness and shortsightedness we so often wish for more than would be good for us. We ask only that thou wilt give us what we need, believing that, if we seek thy good and the good of all, there will be goods enough for all.

...thou dost feed the fowls of the air and clothe the grass of the fields...

Father, thy son has told us that sufficient unto the day is the evil thereof. We would obey him and not borrow troubles from our tomorrows nor fret ourselves about the future. We trust thy promise that as our days

so shall our strength be, and we believe
that thou wilt not burden us beyond what we
are able to bear. And so we now ask only
for that which will sustain us in doing worthily
what this day demands.

When we pray for our daily bread, we mean
more than material good, for Jesus reminded
us that man doth not live by bread alone. We
have learned how true that is, for we recall
times when our bodies were full and our hearts
were empty, and other times when we were
poor in substance and happy in spirit.
The daily bread which we crave from thee
must be food for our souls as well as for
our bodies. And if we have lost our spiritual
hunger, wilt thou arouse our appetite for
the true, the beautiful, the good, and restore
our taste for the simple and the pure.

Give us this day, O God, enough to live for as well as enough to live on, for we need faith great enough to give us purpose, and hope strong enough to give us heart, and love rich enough to give us comradeship.

But as we pray for our daily bread, we are painfully mindful that because we have not put thy kingdom first, multitudes of thy

children are in misery, want, and sin.
Wilt thou, then, "Forgive us our trespasses, as
we forgive those who trespass against us."

We all belong to thy world-wide human
family, and even the best of us must
bear some responsibility for the sins which
beset society. If thy pure son, Jesus of
Nazareth, suffered himself to be baptized for
the sins of his people, how much more
should we feel guilt for the ungodliness around
us. We have gone with the crowd in its
compromises. We have allowed personal comfort
and private interest to keep us silent when
we should have spoken out. We have permitted
lies to pass current in our presence when

"Give us this day our daily bread."

we could have stopped them with the truth.
We have fixed our gaze on great social
evils and failed to do the duties next to us.
We have hated and helped to kill the
sinners in other lands and then kept their

sins. We have let our consciences sleep
while evil has become enthroned in high places
and whole races have been wronged and
nations have drifted into war. Father, forgive
us for our share in public sins.

And when we look at those nearest to us,
we fear that we have trespassed on their
lives. May it be that there is a husband or
wife for whose personality we have lacked
kindly consideration, or a child for whose
opinions we have not had charitableness,
or an aging parent for whose welfare we have
not had concern, or a friend for whose
privacy we have not had respect? May it be
that in our haste we have failed to heed
the hands reached out for help or spurned some
generous offers of aid? May it be that in
our pride we have scorched some humble soul

with scorn, or by our gossip we have
wounded another's reputation, or by our
prejudice we have spread the spirit of
ill will, or in our anger we have sent forth
the sting which we cannot recall? May
it be that with lustful look we have poisoned
the beauty around us, or in our greed we
have lowered the standards of honesty, or by

our indulgence we have profaned bodies
which are the temples of thy Holy Spirit?

Father, forgive us our open sins and
our secret faults. If any brother hath aught
against us, lead us to him that we may
be reconciled. If we have taken love's gifts for
granted, let our thankfulness find ways
of redeeming our thoughtlessness. If we have
grown weary in well-doing and have
disappointed the hopes we raised, forgive our
failure to follow through and help us to
finish what others rightfully expect of us.

We crave thy forgiveness, O God, for though
we try to forget our sins, we cannot forgive
ourselves. When we set our sins in the light of

And when we look at those nearest to us, we fear that we have trespassed on their lives.

thy countenance, we do repent and are heartily sorry for these our misdoings. The remembrance of them is grievous unto us. But when we think of the hours we have wasted and the opportunities we have

forfeited and the blessings we have received
from those no longer present and the
sacrifice made for us by thy well-beloved son,
Jesus Christ our Lord, we know that we
are too deeply in thy debt ever to repay. Only
by faith in thy grace can we be saved.
Only thy forgiving love can blot out our
transgressions and restore our right
relationship.

But, our Father, thy son hath taught us that
we cannot get right with thee unless we
forgive those who trespass against us. Grant
us the spirit of forgiveness, that we may
welcome to our hearts those we have locked
out. Make us magnanimous, too big to be
bothered by little insults or to be embittered by
old grudges. Help us to be well-wishers for
the best interests of all men, that with malice

toward none and with charity for all we may do the right as thou dost give us to see the right.

And, our Father, as we pray for the forgiveness of our past trespasses, we think of tomorrow and also ask, "Lead us not into temptation." We know that thou dost desire our welfare and that thou wouldst not test us with needless trials. When we pray for thy protection against temptation, we believe that we are sharing thy wish for our welfare. We would not presume on thy fatherly goodness by repeatedly and carelessly falling into sin because we can count on thy continuing forgiveness. Keep us mindful that pardon is not easy in a world of justice, that it cost thee a cross to forgive, that we must not treat it lightly.

Lead us, therefore, away from the temptation which caused us to fall yesterday. Help us to say no to the suggestion of evil before the substance of it appears. Let us not look in the direction of our old sins lest

we may walk toward them in our weakness.
Make keen our consciences that we may
catch the scent of sin afar off and cause us to
stop short of the place where temptations
lie in wait for us. Guide our steps along the

paths where we shall think of whatsoever
things are true and honest and pure and lovely
and of good report. Keep us so close to thee
that evil may lose its lure, and take not thy
hand from the helm of our lives lest we
drift into the storms where desire or passion
may prove too great for our strength.

But, our Father, since thou hast created us
free spirits and hast left us to make our
choices in order that we may grow up as thy
children, we needs must face some evils.
We do not ask to be spared the test, but we do
pray, "Deliver us from evil."

Keep us from being overcome by the fear
of evil before we fight it, and let not the
number of wrongdoers hide from our eyes
the legion of those who love the right.

Awaken us to the presence of sins which so often lurk in lovely places and hide behind the second best, but let us not spoil the good by imagining the bad or darken the light of faith with the shadows of suspicion. May we be so pure in our purposes that we shall not impugn the motives of others and may we count on their highest until we bring out their best.

We crave the confidence of him who long ago sang to thee, "I will fear no evil for thou art with me." When other helpers fail and comforts flee, may the sense of thy nearness lift us out of our loneliness and dispel the darkness of fear. We know that if thou art for us, nothing can long stand against us, for no weapon against thee shall prosper. We would remember that what happens to us matters not so much as what happens in us; and that if our heart is fixed on thee, nothing can harm our real selves, for all things work together for good to them that love thee.

We are in bondage to sinful habits which we of ourselves cannot break.

But, our Father, we would be delivered from the evils which we ourselves do. In our own strength we are not equal to the task of being good. The evil that we would not, that we do; and the good that we would, we do

not. We are in bondage to sinful habits
which we of ourselves cannot break. We are
not able to call back the consequences of
our past sins any more than we can recall our
breath. We need thy help to cleanse the
secret chambers of our minds, to pluck from
our breasts the rooted sorrows, and to
renew a right spirit within us. We are not so
craven as merely to seek escape from the
results of our wrongdoing, but we would be
freed from the sins themselves. Break
thou the power of concealed sin and set us
free from the desires which defeat our
good intent. Help us to overcome evil with
good, that we may be more than conquerors
through him that loved us.

Through that love which Christ showed
toward us, we are led to try again and

again when temptation has laid us low. Thou
hast given him unto us as a great High
Priest who was tempted in all points even as
we are, and yet without sin. We believe
that thy son Jesus Christ is our Advocate with
thee, evermore living to make intercession
for us. If we are faithful to him, we know that

we can face the future unashamed and
unafraid. Therefore, through this same Jesus
Christ, who ever reigneth with thee world
without end, we pray, "Lead us not into
temptation, but deliver us from evil."

"For thine is the kingdom." Though we rebel
against thee, thou still dost reign. Though
we deny thy power, thy scepter does not fall.
Though we may doubt thy very being,
thy laws uphold us while we question them.
Though wayward and wicked, we try to
live without thee. Thy rule of righteousness
is within us and around us as the sun
waits for the clouds and darkness to pass away.

Though the love which lay in a manger and hung on a cross looks weak, it is the force which lasts...

"And the power." The heathen rage and the kingdoms are moved, but thou dost count the nations as the small dust of the balance and taketh up the isles as a very little thing. We boast our strength and clash our arms but, when

> The captains and the kings depart;
> Still stands Thine ancient sacrifice,
> An humble and a contrite heart.

Though the love which lay in a manger and
hung on a cross looks weak, it is the
force which lasts and never faileth in the end.

"And the glory." When we behold thy greatness
in all the earth, thy goodness which shineth
through the shadows of sin, thy grace which
redeemeth our lives from destruction, we
are lost in wonder, love, and praise. Thou hast
been our dwelling place in all generations
and art our hope of an eternal home. Therefore
will we not fear though the paths of earthly
glory lead but to the grave, for "Thine is the
kingdom, and the power, and the glory,
for ever and ever."

DESIGN AND ILLUSTRATION: Jean Penland

TYPE: Dolphin
Display, 18 pt., 22 pt., and 38 pt.
Text, 15 pt., leaded 5 pts.

TYPESETTER: Warwick Typographers, Inc.

MANUFACTURER: The Parthenon Press

PRINTING PROCESS: Offset, 2 colors

PAPER: 70 lb. Beckett Text Laid, India
Graham Paper Company

BINDING MATERIAL: Holliston's Natural Finish
The Holliston Mills